Songs and Poems from a Yielded Heart

By
Judith Vander Wege

Songs and Poems From a Yielded Heart will draw the
readers into closer relationships with God as they read
about his comfort and mercy and Lordship.

ISBN: 979-8-8692-9981-9
Company Name: Paper Wrights
Printed in the United States of America,

Table of Contents

Poems Are...

1

Poems are the strivings of the soul

expressing the inexpressible,

understanding the hurts,

finding a way of coping,

making our spirits whole.

The Greater Gift

2

"Lord, give me clear sailing," is what I often cry

when I feel the fog's so thick I'd really rather die.

Then, just for a moment, he'll cause the fog to lift.

And he says, "My grace, sufficient, is the greater gift.

"When at last, you've stood the test," he gently lets me know,

"you'll receive the crown of life. The trials help you grow."

©1977 Judith Vander Wege

Comfort

"Let me sing a song to you. Let me know if you are feeling blue.

Wipe those tears away. Lift your eyes and pray.

I will be your friend, love you till the end.

For I came to save you from the tyranny of sin.

Give your life to me. Life Abundantly is what I will give you

when you trust in me to set you free.

I will wipe away your tears.

Perfect love will cast out all your fears.

Yes, I gave my life, just to end your strife.

When you come to me gold is what I see.

I know you are precious and I want you to be mine.

Clouded now by sin, dirt and dross within,

Yield to my refining.

When the trials are done, how you will shine.

© 1980 Judith Vander Wege

Judith Vander Wege

Prayer of Confusion

Will somebody tell me how to live?

What is the secret? How do I give?

How do I yield my heart?

Will somebody tell me who I am?

Which is the truth and which but a sham?

How did deception start?

What are the answers … I need them now

to questions I can't figure out somehow.

Am I wise or am I a fool? Am I loving or am I cruel?

How do I listen and who will speak?

I feel confused and amazingly weak.

O LORD, take control of my inner soul.

Where I am lacking, please make me whole.

Search me and make me true.

For you are the one who gave me life.

Tell me the secret, thus end my strife. Teach me to live for you.

The Sovereignty of Christ

You are the mighty King, Master of everything.

Though you are gentle, you rule over all.

Why do you plead for me? Why did you bleed for me?

Why bother sending your call?

Your love has reached me and made me complete

so I couldn't resist all the love you did give.

Now I can worship you, Lord of the Universe

as in my heart you do live.

Jesus I love you! I want to obey you

and live in a way that will glorify you.

How can I serve you best? Help me to stand the test.

Thank you for making me new.

You are my shepherd and you're my provider;

you have brought peace to this heart full of strife.

I will obey you, for you are in charge of me.

You are the Lord of my life.

©2007 Words & Music by Judith Vander Wege

Judith Vander Wege

Through The Valley

I felt so all alone, so lost and far from home.

I looked not forward to another day.

I longed for Christ to come. I said, "Please take me home!"

Then Jesus lovingly showed me the way:

"You must go through the valley to get to the other side.

It's lonesome in that valley, but I will be your guide.

I know you feel I'm far away,

that I don't hear you when you pray,

but even in your valley, I am always close to you."

The grief I could not bear without someone to care,

though Jesus promised He'd be by my side.

I could not feel His love; I wanted flesh and blood

and so I took a road that led nowhere.

Then I cried out to God. I sought him in his word;

He said, "My precious child, you are my own.

You need to cling to me. Trust me to set you free.

Just hold my hand and I will lead you home.

Chorus

"You must go through the valley to get to the other side.

It's lonesome in that valley, but I will be your guide.

I know you feel I'm far away,

that I don't hear you when you pray,

but even in your valley, I am always close to you."

So now I praise His name. My Savior, still the same,

has led me forward through the sun and rain.

He's brought me close to Him. He's taught me how to win.

By trusting Him, I've learned to grow through pain.

Chorus

"You must go through the valley to get to the other side.

Its lonesome in that valley, but I will be your guide.

I know you feel I'm far away, that I don't hear you when you

pray, but even in your valley, I am always close to you.

Yes, even in your valleys, I am always close to you.

©1987 Words & Music by Judith Vander Wege

Judith Vander Wege

Healing Elements

8

A soft, gentle breeze caresses my skin,

Uplifting my spirits, it soothes me within.

I gaze at the sunset, with awe contemplate

the marvelous beauty my God did create.

Music is healing, music gives wings

To soar above problems this troubled earth brings.

Lord, You sent the music,

You give the sunsets,

You are the breeze to my soul.

Preview of Spring

Thank you, dear Lord,

for the preview of spring.

Early this morning, I heard a bird sing.

Breezes feel gentle, not blustery cold.

Sunshine and blue skies, precious like gold.

Now the prediction of snow makes us cringe,

However, on springtime our hopes do not hinge.

Jesus, who once stilled the storm, is still here

Telling us all through our lives, "Do not fear."

© 2/22/2017 Judith Vander Wege

Judith Vander Wege

The Arboretum

Brown and yellow pine needles carpet the floor
of the arboretum;
Entwining branches form a ceiling.
The river hums steadily,
accompanying the sporadic melodies of birds.
Lacy pine boughs lend their fragrance
while the breeze whispers secrets of Love.

I drink in nature's sustenance.
Then, strengthened and energized,
I run life's race with joy.

The Saint

A saint is a sinner saved by grace,
salvaged, made worthy to see God's face.

Serving the Lord with a song in her heart,
this steward is faithfully doing her part.

Sometimes a saint will suffer alone,
even rejected by those in his home.

But God has acquitted, adopted this one.
So life is abundant, assured by the Son.

In Christ she abides, invited to stay.
The Lord intercedes for him each day.

Indwelt by the Spirit, reflecting His image,
Saint gains an inheritance kept for his lineage.

No other name could be so adored
as Jesus Christ's name, for He is the LORD!

Neighbors are loved, and God supplies needs.
Thankful saint worships the Lord as He leads.

Judith Vander Wege

Tasting God's goodness, thirsting for more,
Saint trains his children to enter life's Door.

Using her talents, she tells of God's deeds
and trusts in God's triumphs, planting His seeds.

Regarding a Loved One

Though I see no miracles of repentance or change,

Though I see no spiritual fruit,

Though I see no effectiveness of God working through me,

Though the seeds I've planted are not ready for harvest,

Though communication is even cut off

and there's no apparent bond of relationship,

Yet I will rejoice in the Lord.

He is my salvation and my strength.

He gives me success and joy.

©1996 Judith Vander Wege
New application of Habakkuk 3:17-19

Judith Vander Wege

Give Warning!

O Watchman, blow the trumpet!

Don't take your life of ease.

Give warning to the multitude that's trapped by sin's disease.

O Watchman, blow the trumpet.

If you neglect this call, then who will give the message that God's

love is for us all?

O Watchman, blow the trumpet.

Fulfill our Lord's commands. If you do not give warning,

their blood is on your hands.

O Watchman, blow the trumpet, for some will gladly hear

And turn to God for healing. Obey, and bring them near.

Based on Ezekiel 3:17-21 & 33:1-9

I Will Restore You Now

I love you so! You are my Lord! I praise your name! For you have

said to me: "I will restore you now. I'll build you up; I know the

plans I have for you. For you've returned to me,

and I delight in you!"

Once I didn't know, once I didn't see that you came to this earth just

to set me free!

Now I know that you sought me with your unfailing love. With your

blood you bought me. You have called me by my name! You've

blotted out my sins.

I love you so! You are my Lord! I praise your name! For you have

said to me, "You are my precious child. I love you so, my child. I

will restore you now."

©Judith Vander Wege- lyrics 1984, music by Steve Kohl 1984

Judith Vander Wege

Praise For Adoption

When I think of who you are,

I cannot grasp it all.

My mind can't comprehend

the bitterness and gall

your Holy Son, my Lord,

went through to bring me home.

My heart resounds with praise

each time I speak your name.

Almighty, Holy God,

eternally the same,

is named my *Father,* too.

Thanks for adopting me!

Holy Spirit, Dwell In Me

Holy Spirit, dwell in me with your gracious love divine.

Cleanse each sinful, prideful thought that afflicts this soul of mine.

Lead me now to know the will of my Lord who set me free.

Give me pow'r and strength to live. Holy Spirit, dwell in me.

You're my helper, counselor, comforter in all my strife.

Now I thank and praise you, Lord, for you give abundant life.

Lead me now to know the will of my Lord who set me free.

Give me pow'r to overcome. Holy Spirit, dwell in me.

Lord and giver of new life, who proceeds from Father/Son,

You're the guarantee for me that I'll win this race Christ won.

Lead me now to know the will of my Lord who set me free

Give me pow'r to live for Christ. Holy Spirit, dwell in me.

©2011 Words and music by Judith Vander Wege

Someone

Are you out there? The one who is in God's plan for me?

The one to whom I can talk for hours

in a "friendship deep and clean?"

I want to tell you who I am

every corner and hidden closet.

I want to know who you are,

past, present, future dreams and hopes.

If I can give you courage and a joy in living,

and you can give me strength and clarity,

then we can soar together.

Where are you?

Have I met you yet?

Or am I to live for God alone?

©2004 Judith Vander Wege

I am the Ground

The plow cuts deep, again and again and again!
It cuts away my roots, my desire to be 'altogether,'
my desires to look good.
It turns me over, inside out, till I am a mess of crumbly soil.

The rains come; seeds are planted.
I miss the lovely pasture I used to be, with calves frolicking in the sunshine,
butting heads, coming to me for nourishment.
Here I lie, useless and alone—except for this farmer
who constantly runs over me with his tractor, seeding, cultivating.

I am changing.

I finally recognize the farmer.

Lord, do with me as you choose, for I belong to you.
Plant the seeds, cultivate out the weeds, send the sunshine and rain.
Oh Lord of the harvest, may I yield abundantly
for you whatever crop you choose.

Amen

© 2017, Judith Vander Wege

I Am Bethlehem

We expect Christmas to be a joyous time. But for many, Christmas simply intensifies feelings of hopelessness and loneliness.

Many years ago, I struggled with depression as Christmas drew near. Wanting to keep my commitment as a choir member, I forced myself to participate in the Christmas concert. I broke down in tears before we entered the sanctuary. Friends, knowing my situation, hugged me. They gave me strength to compose myself and prepare to sing. As the concert proceeded, I began to listen with my heart to the words we sang:

"O little town of Bethlehem, how still we see thee lie. Above thy deep and dreamless sleep, the silent stars go by; yet in thy dark streets shineth the everlasting light. The hopes and fears of all the years are met in thee tonight."

Dark streets. That sounds gloomy. That sounds like me.

As we went on to the second and third verses, I began to see what God was doing behind the scenes. "Where meek souls will receive Him still, the dear Christ enters in." Suddenly, I sensed that God was speaking to me through the words of the song.

I am Bethlehem!

I thought of the verse in Galatians 4:4, "But when the time had fully come, God sent forth his Son, born of woman, born under the law, to redeem those who were under the law, so that we might receive adoption as sons. And because you are sons, God has sent the Spirit of his Son into our hearts crying, "Abba! Father" (Gal. 4:4-6, RSV).

Between songs, I quickly jotted down my thoughts on my bulletin. By the time the concert was over, I felt more hopeful and less lonely than I had in a long time. God's truth and presence were lighting up my darkness. This poem resulted from that experience.

I am Bethlehem... little, insignificant, inadequate in my eyes.
How long have I lain here still, hoping for a glimmer of Your glory,
going through the motions day after day?
LORD, You gave a promise through prophets long ago.
Will Your promise be fulfilled in me?
Will my purpose be fulfilled?
Above me, the stars are silent. My heart aches with their silence.
I anguish to hear Your voice.
But suddenly! Has the time fully come?
Here You are, shining in the dark streets of my heart,
driving out gloom.
In Your radiance, You speak, giving Your Word flesh!
Therein my hopes are fulfilled, my fears dispelled.
O Glorious LORD! There is room in me for You!
Fill me to overflowing with Your glory!
Shine and speak through me.

Make Your music resound through me that others may know

the song You've given, the peace You have brought.

Is this my purpose?...that You have come to be born in me?

This reminder by the Holy Spirit, that Jesus did indeed come to earth to be "born in me" (i.e. received by me as Savior and LORD) made my troubles fade into insignificance. Like Bethlehem of old, the only significance I need is to be a dwelling place of Christ. He is Emmanuel, God with us in all our problems. He gives us significance, adequacy, hope and comfort. He makes my heart want to sing with the joy of His presence.

The Miracle of Flying

Above the clouds, the sky was blue.

The sun shone bright as on we flew.

How can it be we fly so high,

though gravity would draw us nigh

to dash us to the ground

where we would nevermore go forth to see

the fluffy clouds from up above,

to laugh or think or even love?

Yet on we fly without a care.

We sleep or read, or talk and share.

One day I'll fly above the clouds

without a plane or engine loud.

The Son will shine within my heart

as on I fly. A place apart

to live with him will be my goal,

and Jesus' love will make me whole.

©2017 Judith Vander Wege

Judith Vander Wege

To Him Who Rides Upon the Clouds

To Him who rides upon the clouds,

I lift my voice in purest praise.

I know what e'er He has allowed,

He'll use in love my heart to raise.

For He's forgiven all my sin,

redeemed my soul from death and hell.

In goodness, surely, He provides

all things I need to serve Him well.

And if I seek Him when He hides,

I'll find He's faithful to restore

the joy of His redeeming grace,

the sunshine of His glorious face,

the peace of knowing He is coming.

I'll be with Him evermore.

Inadequacy to Glory

"I have redeemed you...you are precious in my eyes,
and honored, and I love you... everyone who is called by
my name, whom I created for my glory, whom I formed and made,"
(Isaiah 43:1, 4 &7, RSV)

In my valley, vision is limited. High walls rise on
either side. Mountains impassable, immovable, are barriers
to the vistas of inspiration for which I yearn. I long to 'Write
His Answers,' but don't even comprehend the questions. I
cry out for understanding, longing to glorify God in this inadequate
human frame.
"To them God has chosen to make known among
the Gentiles the glorious riches of this mystery,
which is Christ in you, the hope of glory," (Col. 1:27, NIV).

Created for your glory? Oh Lord, do you mean me?
What is there I could ever do to praise the Trinity?
The answer comes slowly, softly, surely:
Cleansed and forgiven by Jesus Christ,
I live by my Lord's power.
His Spirit is at work in me to perfect the
plan of God in my life to write God's messages.
Yes, this human frame is inadequate,

yet Christ in me is God's glory like

the breath of a musician

empowers a woodwind instrument,

like the wind makes the wind chimes sing,

like a light within a lantern dispels the darkness.

Lord Jesus Christ, speak your gospel message to me, shine in me

and through me, empower me by your breathe, play your beautiful

music through me. Amen.

I Cannot Come

Excuses abound for saving face:

They do not know they're losing grace

by saying "I cannot come."

Of course, they mean, "I will not come."

I won't be bothered with taking the time

to relate to you."

And so, with excuses, they sell their soul.

---©2019Judith Vander Wege

Judith Vander Wege

The Spokesman

Assailed by inadequacies, I wonder,
How can I do anything effectively?
Yet, the stars and all creation
praise You without a voice.
Moses, assailed by inadequacies, spoke
because You, Almighty God, made his voice
and called him.
Flawed disciples, filled with your Holy Spirit,
spoke inspired truths.
Lord, You are the potter,
not limited by our imperfections.
You carefully work the clay,
heat, refine, beautify, perfect.
I am your vessel, Lord. You have called me.
You have given me Your Holy Spirit.
Therefore speak through this vessel
as You have ordained.

Come Before Winter

My friend come before winter,

before the ground grows hard and cold,

before the message seems too old.

Come before winter.

My friend, come before winter.

I long to see your smiling face,

I long to share our Father's grace.

It is so lonely in this place.

Come before winter.

Please bring the wisdom of our Lord,

remind me of his love out-poured,

and wrap me in the cloak you've stored.

Come before winter.

Based on the Apostle Paul's words to Timothy in 1 Timothy 4:6-22.

By Judith Vander Wege, 2006

Judith Vander Wege

Silent Guidance

All alone in dark trials, no answers to be found.

Heartbreak and sorrow I did not understand.

Why must children suffer? Why do loved ones die?

Life and death decisions in my hand.

On my knees, Lord, I begged you for guidance and for help.

This awful silence I didn't understand.

Do you hear my prayers, Lord? Do you even care?

In despair I left all I had known.

Now I see that was guidance from Father to his son.

In that new city, you helped me understand.

I learned that you love me! Other Christians care!

Now I can see your guiding hand.

Thank you, oh my Father! You held me close to you!

You loved me when I thought you didn't hear.

All that time, the plan you had for me was coming clear.

Now I praise your name forever more!

Thank you, oh my Father! You held me c lose to you!

You loved me when I thought you didn't hear.

All that time, the plan you had for me was coming clear.

Now I praise your name forever more!

I Have Calmed and Quieted My Soul

How does one calm the turmoil of grief?

Where does one look for that quiet relief,

when the one who is precious beyond all belief

is no longer here in my world?

He lit the spark of hope in my heart,

gave me the courage to make a new start.

We wanted to marry and nevermore part,

uniting in love with our LORD.

Moonlight and stars still soften the night.

Where there's a shadow, there must be a light.

When God is in charge, the future is bright

for God works in all things for good.

How can I know God's purpose for me?

How do I fathom this painful decree?

The plans we had hoped for are never to be.

Yet, Jesus still reigns o'er my soul.

Christ is The One who quiets my mind.

When I forget, He gently reminds

that the purpose of Him who created my kind

is glorious, though not understood.

©Judith Vander Wege

Judith Vander Wege

The Message

When the storms of life surround me
and knock me to the ground,
and I think I can't go on,
Here's the message I have found:
Jesus understands my pain,
lifts me up to walk through rain,
gives me strength to carry on,
turns my troubles into gain.

Life is full of trials here
but give God an open ear.
He would tell you of his love;
trust him now, don't live in fear.
Jesus understands your pain,
lifts us up to walk through rain,
gives us strength to carry on,
turns our troubles into gain.

When I don't know what to do,
when I don't feel close to you,
Jesus comes and talks with me.
With his love he sets me free.

Jesus understand our pain,

lifts us up to walk through rain,

gives us strength to carry on,

turns our troubles into gain.

Judith Vander Wege

Look at Him

When a dark and dreary sky brings a teardrop in your eye,
as you sit and wonder why, look at Him.
If you feel you've lost all hope and you ponder how to cope,
don't just sit around and mope, look at Him.

He is Savior, He is Lord! He fulfilled all righteousness.
He has taught us how to live, He forever longs to bless.
Jesus Christ, Immanuel, is our present healing King.
If you love him, follow him. He's worth more than anything.
All the way may not be bright; I can't set this world aright,
but I'll keep His love in sight, I'll look at Him.

Jesus knows our every fear. He desires to bring us near
and bestow on us His cheer. Look at Him.
When you're feeling mighty old,
choose the one worth more than gold.
Let Him bring you to His fold: Look at Him.

He is Savior, He is Lord! He fulfilled all righteousness.
He has taught us how to live. He forever longs to bless.
Jesus Christ, Immanuel, is our present, healing King.
If you love him, follow Him, He's worth more than anything.
All the way may not be bright; I can't set this world aright. But I'll

keep His love in sight, I'll look at him.

©Judith Vander Wege

Judith Vander Wege

Love Makes Me Soar

What can I do with my memories?
What can I do with my longing to see
you in my dreams.

You touched my life in your pure, sweet way.
Now I can soar o'er the problems
that once dragged me down.

Love makes me soar like a bird!
Love broke the fetters and let me go free.
Love touched my life for a short, sweet time.
Love gave me reason to be.

Now I can see that this span of time
is but a part of a plan so sublime
wrought by my LORD.

He loves me so He revealed you to me,
meaning to heal through your precious
and untainted love.

Love makes me soar like a bird!
Love broke the fetters and let me go free.

Love touched my life for a short, sweet time.

Love gives me reason to be.

(You've been a blessing to me.)

Judith M. Vander Wege

Judith Vander Wege

Now I Will Soar

(A Father's Day Praise Song)

Father, Heavenly Father!

I lift my heart to you in praise this Father's Day.

Father, I call you my Father,

for you've adopted me into your holy family.

Now I will soar on the wings

of the breeze you've created for me

because you love me and hold me close to you.

For you've redeemed me, justified,

sanctified and purified me.

And how I love you, rejoicing in peace you've given to me.

Father, Heavenly Father,

thank you for answering my prayers

the way that you know is best.

Father, I trust you my Father!

You're kind and merciful, tender,

forgiving and patient with me.

Now I will soar on the wings

of the breeze you've created for me,

because you love me and hold me close to you.

For you've redeemed me, justified,

sanctified and purified me.

And how I love you, rejoicing in peace you've given to me.

Now I will soar on the wings

of the breeze you've created for me

because you love me and hold me close to you.

For you've redeemed me, justified,

sanctified and purified me.

And how I love you, rejoicing in peace you've given to me.

Yes, how I love you, rejoicing in peace you've given to me.

©2007 Judith Vander Wege

Judith Vander Wege

MY HEART CAN SING TO YOU

Based on Psalm 30:12

Chorus

My heart can sing to You! My heart can sing to You.

Oh Lord, my God, You've brought me joy.

My heart can sing to You! My heart can sing to You.

Oh Lord, my God, You've brought me joy.

You picked me up from my despair.

You held me safe within Your hands.

You let me know how much You care.

I praise Your name, Lord Jesus Christ!

My heart can sing to You! My heart can sing to You.

Oh Lord, my God, You've brought me joy.

My heart can sing to You! My heart can sing to You.

Oh Lord, my God, You've brought me joy.

You are the Way; You are the Truth.

You are the Breath that gave me life.

You called me close when but a youth,

and taught me how to walk with You.

My heart can sing to You! My heart can sing to You.

Oh Lord, my God, You've brought me joy.

My heart can sing to You! My heart can sing to You.

Oh Lord, my God, You've brought me joy.

© Judith Vander Wege, 1999

Judith Vander Wege

In The Fullness of Time

"Alleluia! Alleluia.

Alleluia! Alleluia, Alleluia."

In the Fullness of time

God has sent forth his Son

whom the prophets foretold, long awaited one.

For we were bound deep in our sin,

darkness had reigned without and within.

We needed light to lead the way.

Jesus has freed us,

he's our hope and stay.

"Alleluia! Alleluia.

Alleluia! Alleluia, Alleluia."

God took on flesh, born as a man,

born to fulfill the heavenly plan.

Jesus atoned for all our sins.

We can be free and pure and whole within.

Now we are free. Jesus our Lord

renews our minds through his holy word.

In all we say, in all we do, let's tell the world,

"He longs to save you, too!"

43

"Alleluia! Alleluia.
Alleluia! Alleluia, Alleluia."

Awesome Love

Hey there! Look around me and see
Someone has so much love for me.
Someone put the birds in the trees.
Someone put the foam on the seas.

Yes, Jesus loves me. (He loves me!)

Yes, Jesus loves me.

Yes, Jesus loves me, the Bible tells me so.

Listen to the song of the birds,

singing praise to God with no words.

Don't you see, it's all in his plan.

God created beauty for man.

Yes, Jesus loves me. (He loves me!)

Yes, Jesus loves me.

Yes, Jesus loves me, the Bible tells me so.

©2017 Judith Vander Wege, verses.

Chorus by Anna B. Warner, 1859

Bring Me to Your Holy Place

Bring me to your holy place,

the place where I can feel your grace.

It's next to you, a place of love and mercy.

Near to your heart, I long to find repose.

Set me now apart to worship you and be restored.

Bring me to your heart. Set me now apart

to worship you and know your grace.

Thank you for your covenant,

the one you have prepared for us.

For by your blood, you've brought us to your Father.

Now reconciled, I put my hope in you.

Strengthen me by grace

To live my life to honor you.

Thank you for your grace,

Thank you for this hope,

That I can live to honor you.

©2017 Judith Vander Wege

Judith Vander Wege

Melchizedek

Melchizedek, oh what a mystery!
Melchizedek, a great high priest was he.

King of Salem, priest of the Most High God,
met Abraham as home from war he trod.
Then this patriarch gave tithes to him,
king of righteousness and king of peace.

Melchizedek, oh what a mystery;
Melchizedek, a great high priest was he.

We know Jesus, Son of the LORD Most High,
became a priest and gave himself to die.
Now Melchizedek resembles Him,
King of Righteousness and King of Peace.

Melchizedek, you're still a mystery.
But Jesus is the great High Priest for me.

by Judith Vander Wege

Metamorphosis

Butterfly, butter fly are you glad you had to die?
Now you're free to fly around as we watch without a sound.

Butterfly, you're just like me.
I have died, now I am free, free to fly as joy abounds.
Left my chains down on the ground.

Just like you, I was bound by my nature to the ground.
But a change has taken place. Jesus freed me by His grace.

Butterfly, you're just like me.
I have died, now I am free; free to fly as joy abounds.
Left my chains down on the ground.

Now with love I abound.
My Lord's grace makes praise resound
May my life cause fruit to grow as I spread God's love below.
Butterfly, you're just like me.
I have died, now I am free; free to fly as joy abounds.
Left my chains down on the ground.

©1981 Judith Vander Wege

Judith Vander Wege

My Valentine to Jesus

Lord, speak to my heart, Lord speak to my dreams.

Let me know of all your plans and schemes.

I long for your touch. You thrill me so much.

Let me know all your will. Stay by me still.

Let me be thine.

You spoke to my heart, began all my dreams.

You have canceled sins and Satan's schemes.

My heart's main desire is walking with you.

Let me know all your will. Stay by me still.

Keep me as thine.

You are Lord of my heart, dear Lord of my dreams.

You've removed from me my foolish schemes.

Now I feel your touch, you thrill me so much!

As we both walk with you, make one from two.

Dear Valentine.

O My Strength

Psalm 59:9-10

Oh my strength, I will sing praises to Thee.

Oh my strength, I will sing praises to Thee.

Oh my strength, I will sing praises to Thee,

for thou oh God art my fortress.

My God in His steadfast love will meet me;

My God will let me look in triumph on my enemies.

For Thou, O God, art my fortress.

I will sing praises to Thee.

©1993 Judith Vander Wege

Judith Vander Wege

King of our Hearts

(Song of the Wise men)

"Why would a star be shining so brightly?
What does it mean? Why does it seem to be singing?
Night after night we've studied the heavens
hoping to learn what is this star's special meaning."

"Friends let me show you and ancient prophecy.
'In the land of Israel a star will soon appear.'
Could this mean a ruler of power and majesty
Comes to set the whole entire world free from sin?

Let's go and find this King of the whole earth,
follow his star, travel afar 'til we find him.
Let's find this King of our hearts.
Yes, Let's find this King of our hearts."

Christ is Born

(After the angels appeared to the shepherds, imagine them singing

this song:

"Let's go and see the baby born there in Bethlehem tonight.

Angels were sent by God above to tell us this good news."

"Let's go and see the baby whom angels said

is Christ the Lord.

They said we shouldn't be afraid

for he will save us from our sins."

"Oh what a thrill it was to see angels in the sky

What joy to know the Lord is nigh!

Now let's hurry!"

"Look. There's the lowly manger—Is that

a baby lying there?"

"Yes, that's the one the angel spoke of,

Jesus Christ the son of God."

"Praise God, we've seen the baby born there

in Bethlehem tonight.

Let's tell the people of the city

Christ was born this day.

So long we all have waited

for Christ the Savior of the world.

Peace, joy and hope now fills our hearts
for he will save us from our sins.

We've seen the lowly manger
Where lies the Savior of the world.
Praise God, he's not forgotten us
for Jesus Christ is born.

©Judith Vander Wege

What Do You Desire?

Lord, you showed love to me when I had no one to turn to.

Lost and alone, so far from home.

Your grace and mercy found me,

you broke the chains that bound me.

Now I long to show my gratitude.

What do you desire? What do you require?

How can I return your love and praise your Holy name?

What's your will for me? Jesus, help me see.

(This is what the Bible says to me):

"The Lord has told you people what he wants from you:

Do what is right to other people; love being kind to them;

live humbly in an obedient relationship with God.

Care for orphans and widows who need help.

Keep yourself free from the world's evil influence.

Feed the hungry; provide pure water for the thirsty;

Befriend the lonely; clothe the refugees; care for the sick;

visit those in prison; pray for those persecuted for their faith."

For Jesus said, "Whatever you do for the least of these,

you do it for me."

© Judith Vander Wege, paraphrases/ Micah 6:8, James 1:27, Mt. 25:34-40

Blessed Be He

Blessed be he. Praise his glorious name.

Blessed be the Lord our God, for he is worthy.

Praise to the name of Jesus Christ,

the one begotten Son of God.

In love, he claimed us as his own adopted ones.

Can you fathom the mystery?

Can you comprehend his love?

How could a holy righteous God,

the great creator of us all,

choose to redeem us, to rescue us in grace?

Oh how amazing! What love, what joy!

That we may live to praise his glorious, holy name.

Praise to the name of Jesus Christ;

we live to glorify his name. In love he claims us,

he loves us as his own.

Oh how amazing! What glorious grace!

Blessed be the Lord our God for he is worthy.

Praise for Rescue

When I think of you I bow my knees.

You are the one who rescued me from sin.

In your grace, you taught me to believe.

Now your Holy Spirit dwells within.

I love you, Lord!

I want to live my life to praise your name.

I praise you, Lord!

I want to spend my life in praising you.

©2017 Judith Vander Wege

Judith Vander Wege

Speechless and Amazed

Father, when I think of your love for me,

Your care, protection and support,

saying thanks to you seems so small.

I'm speechless and amazed that you love me.

Looking at the night sky, I see the stars.

You made them all and know their names.

Every day you give light and warmth.

I'm speechless and amazed that you love me.

Gazing at the beauty surrounding me,

the trees, the mountains and the plains,

When I look at all you have done,

I'm speechless and amazed that you love me.

Father, to say thank you just seems so small,

I yield to you my heart and soul.

I will follow you all my life.

I'm speechless and amazed that you love me.

Son of God, My Savior

You paid the ransom with your blood to set us free,

You welcomed us with open arms and let us be

adopted as your own joint heirs, protected from the devil's snares,

sheltered from the world's worst cares.

Praise God you ransomed me.

How could I not receive your love? You rescued me!

Deception's trap had sucked me in. You salvaged me.

Confusion, loneliness and pride

had tried to drive me from your side.

But in your love I still abide.

By grace, you pardoned me.

Futility would be my lot without your love,

without the constant hope of life with God above.

You turned the light on in my soul.

You cleansed from sin and made me whole.

To love and serve you is my goal.

You liberated me!

©2014 Judith Vander Wege

Judith Vander Wege

I LOVE YOU, LORD

I love you, Lord. You're mine forever.

You're my Redeemer, King and Friend.

You've paid the price; Your blood has saved me.

You gave me life that will never end.

You'll never leave; You'll hold me tight.

The devil's lost, You have won the fight.

What now my Lord? What shall I do

to let you know how much I love You?

You gave me peace that I can't fathom,

an inner joy in the midst of pain.

I want to be Your chosen vessel.

"To live is Christ, and to die is gain."

You'll lead me on o'er land and sea.

To be with You is where I want to be.

I love you, Lord. I'll yield to you.

A yielded life shows that I love You.

Words & Music by Judith Vander Wege, 2004

Author Page

Judith Vander Wege has 300+ credits, mostly in Christian periodicals. Many of the poems in this book were published in Evangel, Live, Power for Living, Standard, War Cry, Hi-Call, Alive for Young Teens, Vision, Purpose, and Grit. She sold other manuscripts to The Lutheran, The Quiet Hour, Foursquare World Advance, Wesleyan Woman, Devotions, The Upper Room, Light From the Word, Bread, Keys for Kids, Harpstring, Christian Library Journal, and anthologies to books: Aglow's *Come Celebrate, Christmas Moments, and Heaven sightings.*

Judith lives in Orange City, Iowa and attends First Reformed Church. She wrote a Topical Bible Study guide for the church to use one year, and has written narratives twice for the annual "favorites" concerts. In past years, the choir has performed two of her musical compositions, and the children's choir performed two others. She also sang in an interdenominational women's chorus and has been a group leader in the community's Coffee Break Bible Study several years. For recreation she likes to read and sleep and take walks.

The children and grandchildren of Judith and her late husband, Paul, live in WA, TX, CA, MI, ID, and IA. So they don't get to see them often enough.

You can contact Judith at her

web page: https://judithvanderwege.com,

or email: judith.vw.4hm@gmail.com

You Tube/Judith Vander Wege